Making Myra

A play by

Pete Hartley

ISBN-13: 978-1-9804-3917-2

Making Myra

A play in one act.

by Pete Hartley

Characters:
Maureen Hindley
Myra Hindley
Ian Brady

Setting:
A cell.

Playing time:
approximately 80 minutes

Cover design based on the premiere poster:
Photograph by Andrew Brindley
Poster graphic by Jim Holland.

.

CONTENTS

ACKNOWLEDGMENTS

This play would not have been comprehensively researched, or written and produced, were it not for the ministrations of my long-time collaborator Andrew Brindley. It would not have been performed so superbly without the talent, temerity and courage of Victoria Glover and the remarkable gifts and relentless grafting of Amy Llewellyn and Alex Kerfoot.

Before embarking on staging the play *uneasy theatre* made a substantial donation to *The Keith Bennett Appeal* which, at the time, was funding the continuing search for Keith's remains.

PH

March 2018

.

This play was first performed
Thursday 14th and Friday 15 April 2011
At *The New Continental* Preston, Lancashire UK.

Produced by **uneasy theatre**

The company was as follows:

Maureen Hindley: Amy Llewellyn
Myra Hindley: Victoria Glover
Ian Brady: Alex Kerfoot

Sound by Andrew Brindley
Lighting by Jennifer Martin
Stage Management by Martha Smith

Directed by Pete Hartley

Setting

A simple, plain minimalistic representation of a cell-like place. The recently deceased form of Maureen Hindley is laid out, covered, on a table. A plain shelf arrangement bears a few items. Two chairs. This is suggestive of a more comfortable prison cell but the depiction is ambiguous rather than definitive. On the shelves are items that will be used as props at various points in the action. They include a packet of cigarettes, an ash tray, an ordnance survey map, a hatchet, a plain brown paper bag containing a selection of gifts, one of which is wrapped, another separate gift about the size of a shoe box and wrapped in Christmas paper (1960s vintage), a pile of newspapers, a set of Rosary beads, a hair brush, a small pile of 7 inch 45 rpm vinyl records, two hardback library books, a flannel and towel, a shaving mirror and razor, a transistor radio (1960s vintage) a black wig, a headscarf, a cosmetic bag (1960s vintage) with lipstick, a pink paper left-luggage ticket (1960s vintage), a travelling rug, an SLR camera (1960s vintage) cleaning cloths, bleach.

The props should be very neatly arranged and spaciously separated creating a mix of nostalgia and anticipation but also suggesting an imposed rigidity.

LX: *The pre-set state is low in intensity and cool. The form of the deceased being the central focus.*

Pete Hartley

SFX: *During the ten minutes prior to curtain up, Albinoni's* Adagio in G Minor *is quietly played.*

Scene One: Maureen

Whilst the music is playing Myra enters and looks at the shrouded form of her sister. The period design of Myra's coat is indeterminate but she has her hair fashioned in her iconic style and beneath her coat she is distinctively dressed in 1960s fashion. She remains there during the following monologue:
LX: *Myra is backlit. Fade the general cover to a slightly lower intensity during which Maureen rises to sit on the table, and begins to fold the sheet that had previously shielded her from view. Then establish the first state, which is just a little more intense than the pre-set gloom, but still retains a cool and limited cover.*
Maureen is dressed and styled in 1960s fashion and appears to be in her twenties.

SFX: *Fade Adagio.*

Maureen: When she saw my corpse, Myra said it was the first dead body she had ever seen. That, of course, were a lie. In June 1957 Myra peered into the open coffin of her friend Michael Higgins. The three of us had the same initials: Michael Higgins, Myra Hindley, Maureen Hindley. Michael were nearly two years younger than Myra and two years older than me. He were just thirteen. On the afternoon of Friday 14th June 1957, he went swimming in the disused reservoir in Melland fields, Gorton. At ten to seven that evening, a police frogman brought him out. Myra had swam with Michael several times, but she weren't there that day. She always felt that if she had been, she might have saved him. The guilt stayed with her for the rest of her life. They became lifelong companions: Myra and guilt.

Maureen places the sheet on the shelf as Myra takes a set of Rosary beads from her pocket.

Myra: His mother took the rosary beads from his lifeless hand, and gave them to me. I was too scared to go to his funeral. He was the first person who had gone from my life for good. Don't be a cretin and think Michael's death had anything to do with my crimes.

She kneels and quietly prays.

Myra: Hail Mary, full of grace, the lord is with thee. Blessed art thou amongst women and blessed is the fruit of thy womb, Jesus. Holy Mary, mother of God, pray for us now and at the hour of our death. Amen.

(*This prayer is repeated but with a slightly different emphasis.*) Hail Mary, full of grace, the lord is with thee. Blessed art thou amongst women and blessed is the fruit of thy womb. (*pause*) Jesus. (*pause*) Holy Mary, mother of God, pray for us now . . . and at the hour of our death. Amen.

LX: *A clearer illumination of Myra and the setting.*

Maureen: So what made you?

Myra: That, Maureen, is a cretinous question.

Maureen: Sticks and stones, sister.

Myra: Bugger off.

Maureen: You can't hurt me now. I'm dead.

Myra: Hurt you? When did I ever hurt you?

Maureen: When did you not? You hurt us all. Me, Mam, Dad, Dave.

Myra: Don't talk to me about fucking Dave.

Maureen: Dave was a hero.

Myra: Not in my eyes. You never saw what I saw.

Maureen: Thank god.

Myra: If your cretinous husband had kept his mouth shut . . .

Maureen: What? How many more, Myra? How many more would there have been? How many more were there?

Myra: Shut up. I thought . . .

Maureen: What?

Myra: I thought . . .

Maureen: What? What did you think?

Myra: I thought we were friends.

Maureen: You have that effect on people, don't you? Making them think you are their friend?

Myra: Stop it.

Maureen: That's why they went with you. They would never have gone with him. Would they?

Myra: Don't even try – all right love? Don't even try. Loads of 'em tried and they've all failed. It can't be done.

Maureen: What can't?

Myra: Deconstructing Myra. It's impossible. Myra is in-deconstruct-able.

Maureen: Prison has learned you some big words.

Myra: What the hell has got into you?

Maureen: Death. Don't you recognise it?

Myra: For Christ's sake Maureen!

Maureen: (*Takes the Rosary beads and replaces them on the shelf.*) Well, Christ and your kid sister. One of us should be able to sort you out.

Myra: God has forgiven me.

Maureen: Have you got that in writing? On the wall is it?

Myra: Right, right. Just leave me alone.

Maureen: Oh no. I'm not going anywhere. I'm dead now. You can bury me Myra. But you can't keep me quiet.

Myra: I don't get this. We got so close again. I was devastated when I heard of your haemorrhage.

Maureen: I know and only 34. You look for a cause: the fags, the booze, hard livin', sleepin in lorry cabs.

All the above. But more likely two decades of folk knowing you are Myra Hindley's sister.

Myra: So that's it.

Maureen: I can't move on, Myra.

Myra: Until you understand?

Maureen: Something like that.

Myra: You're wasting your time.

Maureen: Well we've both got plenty of that.

Myra: I'm sorry I didn't get here before . . .

Maureen: They'd have switched it off any road.

Myra: They must have known I was on the way.

Maureen: They could have waited.

Myra: Yeah.

Maureen: You could have thrown the switch.

Myra: Fuck you, Maureen.

Maureen: You did that a long time ago. Well, sixteen, seventeen years. Lifetime for some people.

Myra: I'm not listening. You are not really here. This is some kind of . . . delusion.

Maureen: Is it? In your head or out of it, I'm not going anywhere. Unless . . .

Myra: Unless what?

Maureen: Well, let's see shall we? Any road – I call the shots from now on. So let's start at the beginning. Dad wasn't the gentlest of folk when he came back from the war, was he?

Myra: I'm not talking about this any more.

Maureen: I don't think you understand, Myra. We talk when I say. Day or night, awake or asleep, alive or dead.

Myra looks at Maureen.

Maureen: So let's start with our Dad.

Myra holds her stare at Maureen for a moment then speaks:

Myra: Everybody hurt kids when I were growing up. It was normal. Kids and wives, we all got a bashing. It's just what folk did. Dad was no different. Don't pin it on him. There is no excuse for what I did.

Maureen: So why did you do it?

Myra: For love. It's that simple. So can we end this?

Maureen: Funny kind of love.

Myra: What other kind is there?

Maureen: The kind that normal people have.

Myra: Who wants to be normal?

Maureen: Me, please. But it's too late now.

Myra: What's the point in being normal?

Maureen: What's the point in owt? There isn't one. Stupid people look for points.

Myra: Is that why you're doing it?

Maureen: There's a difference, Myra, between a point and a reason. Let's go back to Gorton.

Myra: God forbid.

Maureen: Since when did that ever stop you?

Myra: Piss off Maureen, please.

Maureen: Never.

Myra: You can't mean that.

Maureen: Never.

Myra: Stop it, Maureen. I can't have any 'nevers'. Leave me alone.

Maureen: You'll never walk alone, Myra. They'll make sure of that.

Myra: They?

Maureen: They. I'm taking you back Myra.

Myra: I'm not going back.

Maureen: Gorton. Friday 14th June 1957, the disused reservoir in Melland fields. Ten to seven that evening, a police frogman brings Michael Higgins out.

Myra: Michael Higgins has got nothing to do with this.

Maureen: What if he'd lived, Myra? What if Michael had lived?

Myra: Michael wasn't . . anything. We were just pals. He was always bullied until I stuck up for him. I bullied the bullies. We just went round together. Back streets, Belle Vue.

Maureen: Melland Res.

Myra: The res was the best. Because it was dangerous. And forbidden. The water was deep and cold as a corpse. People went there to die. Terminus for the suicidal. Jenny Green-teeth could drag you under.

Maureen: But you didn't go with him that day. And Michael was drowned. Where was Myra when he needed her? Jenny Green-teeth got him. Pulled him under. Filled his mouth with mud.

Myra: Shut up.

Maureen: Very peaty. East Manchester mud. Sometimes coal slack-black, sometimes dishwater brown. Colour of your hair. 'Till you went all Marilyn. Peroxide blonde. The start of another fixation: bleaching agents. (*She sings*:) Gonna wash that guy right out of my hair. (*She starts fussing with her sister's hair.*)

Myra: For fuck's sake.

Maureen: That's why most girls did it.

Myra: Well you put your shift in.

Maureen slaps Myra across the face.

Maureen: That's what Mam's did. She said you looked cheap.

Myra: Well I wasn't was I? I only ever slept with one man.

Maureen: That's a lie. You slept with a bloody copper. And he was married. And that was after you met Ian.

Myra: What's done is done. It can't be undone. Why do we have to go over it again?

Maureen: To understand.

Myra: It can't be understood.

Maureen: It has to be.

Myra: Do you understand everything you do? Everything you've done? Does anyone? I don't. I don't understand it. I don't understand me. And do you know what Maureen: I'm the one who has to live with me. Day in day out. In this life and the next. For ever, and ever, amen. And I've lived a long time with me now. I know me better than anybody. But if you ask if I understand me, or understand what I did, or understand why I did it, then no I don't. I don't expect I ever will. Perhaps I am just plain evil? Perhaps that's what evil is: me. Just my luck eh? To be born evil. Fate. Destiny. What God wants. And if that's what he wants I haven't got much say in it have I? If I'm the way he wanted me to be, then that's what I have to be.

Maureen: You can't blame it on God Myra.

Myra: Then who can I blame it on?

Maureen: How about Ian Brady?

Myra: Ian didn't make me what I am.

Maureen: Didn't he?

Myra: Would he have made you? Eh? Would he have made you do what I did?

Maureen: No he bloody wouldn't.

Myra: Even if you'd been in love with him?

Maureen: I wouldn't have been in love with him.

Myra: Well I was. From the moment I first met him.

Maureen: I wish you'd never have taken that job at Millwards. I wish you'd never have met him. What about you? (*Pause*) Myra? (*Pause*) Well?

Myra: Well what?

Maureen: Do you wish you'd never met him?

Silence. Then Maureen starts to softly, menacingly, sing Always Something There to Remind Me, as she collects the 45rpm records from the shelf and passes them to Myra.

Maureen: *Sings:*

I walk alone the city streets you used to walk along with me

And every step I take recalls how much in love we used to be

Oh, how can I forget you

When there is always something there to remind me

Always something there to remind me

I was born to love you, and I will never be free
You'll always be a part of me

As Maureen sings, Myra sorts through the singles that Ian gave her to mark each killing.
Maureen: So, let's talk about Ian.

Scene two: Ian

Myra removes her raincoat revealing that beneath she is styled in 1963 fashion. She establishes a simple office space. Ian enters and stands at the shelves fiddling with the radio. He is dressed in a cheap but smart suit, white shirt and plain tie.

Myra: He wasn't interested to begin with. For a whole year. I fell in love with him when I first saw him. Before I saw him. Is that possible? Yes. I did it. We did the impossible me and Ian. But at first he ignored me. Or pretended to. Except when he gave me dictation. He liked to dictate.

Ian crosses and enters the office space.

Ian: Take a letter Miss Hindley.

Myra: Yes Mr. Brady. Occasionally he would give me the eye, but he was just teasing. For a whole year he kept me on the hook. Yet I really wanted him.

Myra takes up two books from the shelf as if from a public library.

Myra: In the end it was his love of words that snared him. I suddenly realised how I could catch him. I went to Gorton Library and borrowed a copy of *The Collected Works of William Wordsworth*, and then *Songs of Innocence and Experience* by William Blake.

Brady What's that book, Miss Hindley?

Myra: Songs of Innocence.

Ian: And Experience. William Blake. Do you like poetry Miss Hindley?

Myra: You'd be surprised at what I like, Mr Brady.

Ian: Would you like to go to the *Three Arrows* in Gorton Lane for a drink and a think?

Myra: I think I would.

Ian: Good.

Myra: And that was it: the point of no return. I had him. I caught Ian Brady with songs of innocence.

Ian: I'm a man of extremes Miss Hindfley.

Myra: Myra.

Ian: Do you like extremes, Myra?

Myra: Why don't you try me?

Ian: You'll have to matriculate.

Myra: Could you spell that word please Mr. Brady?

Ian: M–a–t–r–i–c–u–l–a-t-e. Matriculate. Pass the tests. Just how much dictation can you take?

Myra: Do your worst.

Ian: Oh – I will. (*He fiddles with the radio again*)

SFX: *Excerpt from* The Goons.

Myra: For our second date we went to the pictures to see the biblical epic *King of Kings*.

Maureen: It was *Judgment at Nuremburg*.

Myra: It was *King of Kings*.

Ian: It was *Judgment at Nuremburg*.

Myra: That night, on Gran's lumpy settee we French-kissed like half-starved hyenas, and thumped the virginity out of each other.

Ian and Myra engage in eager and rough foreplay culminating in Ian slapping Myra violently, before he exits.

Maureen: Violent was it?

Myra: Ian never understood the difference between sex and violence.

Maureen: I saw it. I saw the bruises, love. Through the make-up.

Myra: That wasn't the half of it. Some days I daren't go to work, daren't leave the house. And worse than that was the stuff that left no marks at all. But I didn't care. I loved him whatever he did.

Maureen: What did he do?

Myra: It doesn't matter.

Maureen: We'll be the judge of that.

Myra: (*She stares at Maureen. She is disturbed for a moment but then says calmly:*) It was just a test. He was testing me, and I passed.

Maureen: Tell me what he did.

Myra: Pass us a fag. What's it to you?

Maureen: (*Passes the cigarettes.*) We need to know.

Myra: (*Another slight hesitation then:*) Why?

Maureen: What you did, damaged all of us.

Everybody.

Myra: Just leave it.

Maureen: It can't just be left.

Myra: Why not?

Maureen: It puts pictures in the mind Myra, and those pictures can never be wiped away. They can't be hidden in suitcases in railway stations. They are luggage that can't be left in left luggage. Do you get me? Do you get what I'm saying? You're one of us Myra, and what you did we . . .   So we need to know what things was done to you.

Myra: Who's 'we', Mo?

Maureen: Well who do you think? Plus me, and me, and me, and me, and me, and me.

Myra: What the heck are you talking about?

Maureen: And everybody who knows me, and everybody who hears my name, or sees me in a book, or backlit under a wig on telly. Everybody who spat at me. Everybody who put dog-shit through our letter box. Or chucked petrol at our house. We all want to know Myra. Or at least I do. Because then I can go back and tell them to leave me alone.

Myra: Did Dave ever do it to you up your arse, Maureen?

Maureen: No.

Myra: And when he'd done it to you in the right place, did he ever stay in there, and then piss? Did he piss in your ear? Up your nose? In your mouth?

Maureen: No.

Myra: No. But let me tell you, if he had done those

things to you, and no matter what else he did, and no matter how much you loved him in spite of all that, let me tell you what it wouldn't have done. It wouldn't have made you kill children. All right? Happy now?

SFX: *Very brief excerpt from* The Goons. *(A single line gag or similar).*

Ian enters.

Myra: Happy now?
Ian: What's happy got to do with anything? No one with any intelligence wants to be happy.
Myra: Why do you strangle me so much?
Ian: I'm practicing.
Myra: What?
Ian: *(Grabs her and starts to strangle her.)* I'm practicing.
Myra: Get . . . . off! Get off you . . . fucking bastard!
She forces her way free and moves away.
Ian: Where are you going?
Myra: To wash my mouth out.
Ian: Myra.
Myra: What?
Ian: You're very special. Don't be long. Kiddo.
Myra: I won't. Neddie.

SFX: *Excerpt from* The Goons. *This evolves into a radio broadcast of* Housewives' Choice. *The signature tune:* In Party Mood *by Jack Strachey which continues under the* *following . . .*

Myra gets a flannel and wipes her face, neck and ears. Ian visits the shelves and collects a cut-throat razor and shaving bowl and then carefully shaves as if looking in a small mirror between him and the audience. Meanwhile Myra applies her make-up.

Ian: *(Shaving)* We could rob a bank. You could be bonnier than Bonnie and I could sail a yacht up the Clyde. The challenge is to commit the perfect crime. And the way to do that is to write lists.

Myra: What?

Ian: The secret is in the planning. But not planning one. Planning two: the clean-up.

Myra: The clean up?

Ian: Any cretin can plan a crime. The genius plans the clean-up. You strike me as a very clean person, Myra.

Myra: The first day we met I noticed how perfectly manicured your fingernails were.

Ian: I like to keep my hands clean. I like my shirts clean. If clothes are not perfectly clean, there's only one place for them.

Myra: Where's that?

Ian: The fire.

Myra: The fire.

Ian: I want to commit the perfect crime. I want to do something really bad.

Myra: Robbery?

Ian: Murder.

Myra: Murder?

Ian: Murder.

Myra: Who?

Ian: What does that matter?

Myra: Anybody?

Ian: I don't care who I kill, Myra. What matters is that I do the killing.

Myra: Why?

Ian: To prove that I can.

Myra: To prove it to who?

Ian: Whom.

Myra: To prove it to whom?

Ian: To me. Who else?

Myra: To me.

Ian: Aye. To you. But most of all to me. What do you think about that Miss Hindley?

Myra: I think you are a remarkable man, Mr. Brady.

Ian: Let's prove it.

SFX: In Party Mood *by Jack Strachey* (Housewives' Choice *Theme*)

Scene Three: Pauline

Maureen: You hadn't passed your test had you Myra?

Myra: Course I had.

Maureen: Not your driving test.

Myra: I could drive.

Maureen: But we knew her. We both knew her.

Myra: I didn't know it was her when I stopped the van.

Maureen: But when you stopped it. Then you saw it was her. Pauline. Pauline Reade. You could have driven on.

Myra: I couldn't. Ian had flashed the headlight on his bike. It was the signal. If I'd have gone against him, then it would have been me not her.

Maureen: But Pauline. Pauline Reade.

Myra has slipped via her stare into a kind of trance.

Myra: I knew she'd get in the van. It would be easy.
I knew if I could do it to her without conscience, then
I could do anything. (*She speaks as if directly as if to
Pauline*:) Want a lift? Mmm that's lovely perfume. Is
it Saville's June? It's lovely. I've lost a glove. Sounds
daft I know. But it's kid leather. Ian bought it me. I
really want to find it? Mind if we take a short detour?
I think I dropped it at the edge of the moor. Don't
mind do you? Only take us ten minutes.

SFX: *Maureen sings an excerpt from* It's All Over Now
Baby Blue *(Bob Dylan)*

The highway is for gamblers, better use your sense
Take what you have gathered from coincidence
The empty-handed painter from your streets
Is drawing crazy patterns on your sheets
This sky, too, is folding under you
And it's all over now, Baby Blue

SFX: *Ambient sound of Saddleworth Moor.*

Myra: You sure it was a motorbike? Good God,
there's someone coming towards, us. No, it's all right,
it's all right. I can see who it is. It's Ian. God, what a
surprise, it's Ian. He must be looking for the glove
too. Well, let's see if he's found it. How much
perfume have you put on? Hell it's strong. Nice
though. And what a lovely locket. (*Sudden change*:) But
you'll not be needing that where you're going.

LX: *Myra reaches out towards the auditorium and is thrown
into sharp silhouette and then near darkness as Maureen sings*

again:

Leave your stepping stones behind, something calls
for you
Forget the dead you've left, they will not follow you
The vagabond who's rapping at your door
Is standing in the clothes that you once wore
Strike another match, go start anew
And it's all over now, Baby Blue
LX: *Re-establish general cover.*

Maureen: But it were Pauline Reade.

Myra: Ian took her.

Maureen: No, Myra. You took her.

Myra: Took her out of sight. I waited with the van.

Maureen: You could have driven off. Got help.

Myra: We'd already driven off.

Maureen: You what?

Myra: Driven off the planet.

Maureen: What you talking about?

Myra: As of that night, we were no longer of this
world, Maureen. I can't tell you how good that felt.

Maureen: Are you being serious?

Myra: Deadly.

Maureen: Myra.

Myra: We carved our names on the tree of life and
death. They'll still be there in fifty years.

LX: *Ian appears above and behind her, spot-lit and holding a
soiled spade.*

Ian: I've killed three, Myra.

Myra: Three?

Ian: That girl, your soul, and God.

SFX: Ken Thorne and his Orchestra: *Theme from The Legion's Last Patrol.*
Myra and Ian clean up the evidence.

Ian: I have never experienced the need to corrupt anyone. I simply offer the opportunity to indulge extant natural urges. Everybody wants to kill. It's there, inside you. Extant. It exists. The urge to kill exists. It's there inside you, now. Dormant. Sleeping. Don't think you haven't got it. You have. Couldn't harm a fly? That depends on the fly. If it's do or die, then it's goodbye fly. If you have to do it, then take the trouble to do it properly. If I do that it's called murder. If a hypocrite does it, it's called the Death Penalty.

Myra: Did you rape her?

Ian: Get that clean. Then get undressed.

SFX: *Gene Pitney:* Twenty-four Hours from Tulsa.
After a few bars fade low under:

Maureen: Did you always have sex afterwards?

Myra: Don't turn it into something kinky.

Maureen: Wouldn't dream of it. Perfectly normal behaviour.

Myra: Death is a divine intimacy. Ian had killed God. That left a vacancy.

Maureen: You can't mean that.

Myra: Ever made love to a man who could do anything?

SFX: *Restore* Twenty-four Hours from Tulsa.

Scene Four: John

During the song Myra pulls on a black wig, then puts a headscarf over it fastening it under the chin. She re-applies her lipstick. Then she links arms with Ian as if they are a contented couple. The song ends or is faded out.

Maureen: And so to Saturday November 23rd 1963. John Kilbride.

They speak as if to a child positioned between them and the audience.

Myra: You're out late for such a young lad, aren't you?

Ian: I imagine your Mammy'll be worried. We've got children. We worry.

Myra: Want a lift, love? We'll take you home.

Ian: Safely home.

Myra: We've won a bottle of sherry. You can have it

if you like. Present for your Mam. Put her right after all the worrying she'll be doin'. Our car's over here. We'll nip to our house and get that sherry for you. Oh - I've lost a glove. Perhaps you can help us find it? Leather glove. Very fond of it I am. I think I must have dropped it on our way back from Huddersfield. We stopped just on the edge of the moor. Only take us ten minutes. You'll be much better at finding it than we would be. Kids are always better at findin'. What do you reckon? Give you that sherry. If you help us. If you do what we want, we'll give you a reward. Come on. You'll be all right with us.

Maureen sings again:

The highway is for gamblers, better use your sense
Take what you have gathered from coincidence
The empty-handed painter from your streets
Is drawing crazy patterns on your sheets
This sky, too, is folding under you
And it's all over now, Baby Blue

LX: *After this Ian is silhouetted again. He holds the spade in one hand and shakes his fist at the sky.*

Ian: Take that you bastard!

Myra: He was angry at himself. For acknowledging God's existence.

Maureen: Where were you Myra?

Myra: I stayed with the car.

Maureen: The van?

Myra: The car. The Ford Anglia.

Maureen: Where were you Myra?

Myra: I stayed with the car.

Maureen: Did you?

Myra: You know I did.

Maureen: This isn't about knowing. It's about hearing.

Myra: I stayed with the car. Ford Anglia. We went back to Gorton and cleaned it. The news on the telly was full of it.

Maureen: Full of what?

Myra: The killing. Of Kennedy. JFK shot dead in Dallas. Everybody remembers where they were that day.

Ian: We've done it. We've killed a kiddy. Not for politics, not for revenge, just for the hell of it. We've crossed the Rubicon. No return.

Myra: Ian gave me a record to mark the achievement. Gene Pitney: *Twenty-four hours from Tulsa*.

Maureen: Liked his sounds, Ian, didn't he just? Eh? The *Goons*. Hitler speeches. Records. Tapes. The sound of the wind across Saddleworth Moor. Railway stations.

SFX: R*ailway station circa 1963.*

Ian: The steam locomotives. The bustle of folk going about their mundane pointless lives with such moronic urgency. The sound of the romance of the humdrum. It's so sweet when you know you are not part of it. The music of the engineered gargantuan moving monoliths of locomotion. Industrial technology in excess, manufactured to wearily haul the miserable menial to and from their sorry suburban hovels. The sound of steam, the smell of vaporised coal, the feel of worn, third class leather. The satisfying texture of a left luggage receipt. A slip of pink paper that says no one has secrets like mine.

SFX: *Station acoustic fades.*

Myra: No one had secrets like him.

Maureen: Except you.

Myra: Except me.

Maureen: Was that the kick?

Myra: Kicks! (*Sneers:*) Hmm! Kicks don't last. Kicks wear off. This was for ever. The secrets were ours and we were the secrets. We had become the secret.

Maureen: Until you were caught.

Myra: Doesn't change anything. And we weren't caught: we were betrayed.

Maureen: You betrayed yourself Myra.

Myra: That's your opinion.

Maureen: No. It's my observation. But not all of you. There are still secret parts of you.

Myra: Everyone is entitled to secrets.

Maureen: Not your kind of secrets.

Maureen takes up and examines an ordnance survey map of Saddleworth Moors.

Scene Five: Keith

Maureen: Let's talk about Keith.

Myra: Which Keith?

Maureen: Let's talk about Keith, Myra. Where is he?

Myra: How should I know?

Maureen: Don't be a pain, Myra. Where is he?

Myra: Can't you see him from where you are?

Maureen: Not without your help.

Myra: What?

Maureen: Can you see him?

Myra: No.

Maureen: Do you get bad dreams?

Myra: What's it to you?

Maureen: I'll be in there now. Awake or asleep.

Myra: Fuck off will you?

Maureen: In your dreams.

Myra: I've had enough of this.

Maureen: Where d'you bury him?

Myra: (*Sighs heavily, pauses, then:*) I'm not going to tell you Maureen. So you can stop asking.

Maureen: But you know don't you? You know exactly where.

Myra: It all looks the flaming same. I'm a serial killer not a landscape gardener.

Maureen: Serial? How many exactly?

Myra: Leave off. It's just a phrase. You know what phrases are, Maureen. Strings of words.

Maureen: Piss off.

Myra: You should have tried it Mo. Bit of serial killing is a sure-fired route to self-improvement. Prison is a perpetual university. Fast track to a long slow education. I've a got a degree.

Maureen: And now you are officially clever do you think you're a psycho?

Myra: No Maureen. I'm not.

Maureen: Ian is.

Myra: I'm not qualified to judge.

Maureen: Mind you, I knew that the day I met him. I didn't need a degree to work that out. I could sense it. I think you did too. I think that's why you went for him. It was your killer instinct.

Myra: You do talk some crap.

Maureen: He was your James Bond on a bike. From Glasgow with love.

Myra: I've had enough of this.

Maureen: Me too. But it's not over. There's no peace. Don't kid yourself, love. No peace.

Myra: Yeah? Well that's your opinion.

Maureen: And your fault.

Myra: Do you think I wanted it? Do you think I wanted this? Do you think I wouldn't rather be any other human being than the one I was born? But what say did I ever have in that? I was born Myra Hindley, well thank you God. Next time round can I please be oh-so-good Ghandi? Nelson bloody Mandela? Mother fucking Teresa? Anybody except Myra serial killer Hindley, born 23rd July 1942, Crumpsall Hospital.

Maureen: And can I please not be your sister?

Myra: No choice Mo. We all do a life sentence, starting the day we are born. For some it's a holiday camp, for others it's a labour camp. We don't get to choose.

Maureen: You've had your choices. You still have. You can choose to tell me about Keith.

Myra: It's a Greek tragedy. Fate and destiny. Nothing you can do about it.

Maureen: Keith. Keith Bennett. Went to stay the night with his Gran. Never got there. His Mum went to play Bingo. She didn't get lucky that night did she? Do you ever think about her Myra? Do you ever think about any of them? The ones that didn't die. The ones that had to live with what you left them.

Myra: He's somewhere near Shiny Brook.

Maureen: Somewhere? It's a long brook.

Myra: That's all I know.

Maureen: How did you kill him?

Myra: I wasn't there. Ian did it by himself.

Maureen: That's what you always say.

Myra: I know where I was.

Maureen: You was with him.

Myra: Ian killed Keith. Ian buried the body.

Maureen: Oh yeah - and you just hung around and picked wild flowers?

Myra: Ian buried him. Then he came back for me and he kept walking until he stopped to bury the spade. Then we went back to the car.

Maureen: Ford Anglia?

Myra: Mini Traveller. June 1964.

Maureen: Two months before you refused to come to my wedding.

Myra: I don't believe in marriage, and I don't like your choice in men.

Maureen: That's rich, coming from you.

Myra: You were eight months pregnant.

Maureen: Seven.

Myra: Any road, we came round that night. Had a few drinks. We were all right after that weren't we? We are now aren't we?

Maureen: I was seven months pregnant. If I'd have known then what you had done I wouldn't have let you anywhere near me or our Dawn. I shudder when I think how folk trusted you with their kids. They used to say how good you were. How you had a way with them. Not wrong were they? No harm came to kids after you'd taken care of 'em.

Myra: Sarcasm is the lowest form of wit.

Maureen: Well that's about right then isn't it? Since

we're the lowest form of life. Can't get much lower than a Hindley. Apart from a Brady. What did he give you? For Keith.

Myra: Roy Orbison.

SFX: *Roy Orbison:* It's Over. *Play a key phrase then fade but keep under.*

Maureen: Tell me where Keith is.

Myra: I can't.

Maureen: So you're sticking to your story then?

Myra: It's not a story.

Maureen: The SS defence. Keeping guard. Doing what you were told. Just obeying orders.

Myra: It was them or me.

Maureen: That's right. You were their only chance. They haven't forgotten that. And they won't let you forget.

Myra: This conversation is at an end.

Maureen: It's not a conversation. And it won't end it. Tell me where Keith is.

Myra: I wasn't there!

Maureen: All right then: let's talk about Lesley.

SFX: *Fade up the Orbison again and play more, as Ian and Myra wrap up in overcoats and share a travelling rug. They huddle close. Then cross-fade song out and moor acoustic.*

Scene Six: Lesley Ann

Ian: Well, it's gone midnight. Merry Christmas Myra.

Myra: It's freezing. And since when did you believe in Christmas?

Ian: It's for kids, Christmas. That's why I've brought you up here. To be with our kids.

Myra: Why is it called Hollin Brown Knoll?

Ian: We'd need a geographical lexicographer to solve that one.

Myra: The reservoir looks like it's made of quicksilver.

Ian: Mercurial.

Myra: What does that mean?

Ian: Lively, witty, vivacious, likely to do the unexpected.

Myra: That's you then.

Ian: Messenger of the gods: Mercury.

Myra: 'Tis you.

Ian: I only ever bring bad news. And gifts. (*He produces a brown paper carrier with several items inside.*) Presents for you. Pair of kid gloves. Box of Black Magic. Bottle of Sherry.

Myra: You are supposed to wrap them.

Ian: I wrapped this one. (*Takes it from the bag.*)

Myra: (*Unwraps a 7 inch vinyl record.*) Sandie Shaw.

Ian: It's her latest. *Girl Don't Come.*

Myra: Here's one for you. (*She gives him a wrapped gift about the size of a large shoe box and quite heavy.*)

Ian: (*He starts to unwrap it and soon catches on to what it is.*) How could you afford this?

Myra: Ian, don't even think about that. I know how much you want one.

Ian: A tape recorder.

Myra: A good one. Latest thing that. According to the man in the shop.

Ian: Did he have a white beard and a red suit and bounce you on his knee and say ho, ho, ho?

Myra: Got you some other stuff, but it's back at our house. These gloves are lovely.

Ian: Mind you don't lose one.

Myra: (*Sniggers once.*)

Ian: I want to do another.

Myra: Do you?

Ian: I'm ready to do another.

Myra: Today? Christmas day?

Ian: No.

Myra: Thank God for that.

Ian: Tomorrow.
Myra: All right.
Ian: Girl this time.

SFX: Sandie Shaw: *Girl Don't Come.*

Maureen: Lesley Ann Downey.
Myra: I don't want to talk any more.
Maureen: Where were you this time Myra?
Myra: For Christ's sake Mo, can't you just leave it?
Maureen: No, Myra. I can't. Could you?
Myra: What's the point? Where is all this leading?
Maureen: From the Boxing Day fair at Ancoats, to the bedroom at Wardle Brook Avenue.
Myra: I just want to . . .
Maureen: What? Go home? Back to Mam?
Myra: Stop it.
Maureen: Look around Myra. There must be something you can use.
Myra: What for?
Maureen: To stuff into my mouth. To gag me with.
Myra: Bitch.
Maureen: You'll have to do better than that, after what I've heard these last fifteen years.
Myra: Maureen!
Maureen: She was ten, Myra. She was ten. It was Christmas. Boxing Day. And we can hear you on that tape you made . . .
Myra: I didn't make it.
Maureen: . . . stuffing somat in her mouth and

telling her to shut up, so that he could take his sick snaps and then . . .

Myra: I don't understand why we're doing this now.

Maureen: Well we are.

Myra: You've been such a love these last few years, I thought, I thought . . .

Maureen: Well, you thought wrong.

Myra: Why?

Maureen: You can't pretend you weren't there this time Myra, because we can all hear you.

Myra: Not all, not all . . .

Maureen: We can hear you helping him.

Myra: Not when he, not when he . . .

Maureen: Oh don't even bother Myra. You were at all of them. You were there. You were there.

Myra: Not when he . . .

Maureen: As if that matters! You never married him, but you can never divorce yourself from what he did. Every sick bit of it. Every sick bit.

Myra: He made me.

Maureen: Perhaps you wanted to be made? They couldn't escape, Myra, but you could. All you had to do was tell me.

Myra: I'm telling you now.

Maureen: Too late, love, too late.

Myra: Then why the hell do you need to know?

Maureen: You really don't get this do you?

Myra: No. I don't.

Maureen: And I'm supposed to be the thick one.

Myra: Then explain to me. Why do you need to

know?

Maureen: I don't. They do.

Myra: Who?

Maureen: And so do you.

Myra: What?

Maureen: They'll be here soon.

Myra: Who?

Maureen: They're coming to see you Myra.

Myra: Who are?

Maureen: They're quite close now.   They'll soon be with us. And then you will have some explaining to do. (*She sings:*)

All your seasick sailors, they are rowing home

All your reindeer armies, are all going home

The lover who just walked out your door

Has taken all his blankets from the floor

The carpet, too, is moving under you

And it's all over now, Baby Blue.

Maureen: You had your secrets. You'd become the things you'd done. You'd done the worst you could do. Why did you have to do more?

Scene Seven: Edward

Myra: Ask David Smith.

Maureen: That's all you ever said, after you were arrested: ask David Smith.

Myra: We'll he betrayed us. Him and you.

Maureen: You betrayed yourself Myra, the first time you stopped your little car and opened the door for Pauline Reade.

Myra: It's impossible to betray yourself. What ever you do is what you do. It's you. That's all. It's you. It's who you are.

Maureen: Yes.

Myra: It's who I was. Who I am. I could do it, David Smith couldn't. He spent hours talking to Ian. Listening to Hitler. Ian was testing him, just like he tested me. That's why we got him round that night.

Ian enters as if talking to David.

SFX: *Hitler rally. Continue under . . .*

Ian: What would you do David, if someone obstructed us? We'd have to use the firearms David, to remove the obstruction. How would you feel about that?

Maureen: Dave is very easily led.

SFX: *Boost Nazi rally for a few moments then fade out.*

Ian: I've got an admission to make David.   I've killed people.

Maureen: Dave told me he thought it was the beer talkin'.

Ian: Three. Or more. Maybe four?   I could make it five. You don't believe me do you, David?   Well - patience. Patience is a virtue. And I don't have a lot of virtues. But I am patient. I can be patient. I can endure. I can tolerate time. You know why? Because I am unfamiliar with boundaries. I don't have limits. There are no extremes beyond which I cannot go.   Ever been beyond the unthinkable David? I can take you there. But only if you can stand being there. Is there anything you wouldn't do, David? No – don't say. If you say it, you impose it. You set your own limits. So keep silent, because silence knows no limits. Beyond the edge of silence there is simply more silence. The rest is silence. Can you swallow the silence David? Can you face endless silence and keep your peace? The perfect crime is one thing, but the perfect crime can be surpassed by the donation of the perfect gift. And the perfect gift is silence. I have given that gift four times. There will be a fifth. It will be done.

Maureen: I told Dave to have nowt to do with him, and I didn't like it that he were with you. But Dave were taken in by him.

Ian: The people I've killed, they're all under twenty-one. The police, in their institutionalised ignorance, don't pay much attention to missing reports of people under twenty-one. They go missing all the time. Sometimes I just wait in the car, pick people up, give them a lift. Hitching. Bit of a hitch David: a knife to the throat. Bit of a hitch.

Maureen: Dave laughed when I warned him.

Ian: Strangulation feels the best. It's the way the big cats kill. They clamp the windpipe and suffocate their panting prey. Lions do it that way. The lion, or the lioness. The tiger, the jaguar, the leopard. Next time, I'm going to do it like a man. Axe to the head. (*He take a hand axe from the shelf and swings it in rehearsal of what he might do.*)

Maureen: When he told me what had happened at your house it was like he'd hit me with a bloody axe.

Ian: I like to kill in our house. That way you can clean everything up to perfection. Burn and bleach.

With an axe, Dave, with an axe. (*He swings the axe again.*) I take Pro-plus. It's a stimulant. I take Pro-plus before and I take photographs afterwards. So I can prove it.

Maureen: So he could re-live it.

Ian: Then I bury them on Saddleworth Moor. Sacred place, David. A sacristy of crime. People walk there. Take the air, exercise their dogs, take their snaps and savour the views. They don't know they're standing on a cemetery.

Maureen: I reckon your Ian could see my Dave didn't believe him so that's why he went for Edward Evans.

Myra: The car in front of us hit a dog. We stopped. It was awful, and we offered to take it to the vet's, but it just got up and was all right, so we just comforted the owners. Ian had given me another record that morning Joan Baez: *It's All Over Now Baby Blue.* I was scared that Ian was going to do me next.

Maureen: Why would he do that?

Myra: If David Smith turned out to be a better partner in crime, he might get rid of me. And he probably couldn't think of a better felony to test himself. If he could love me and kill me and feel no regret then he'd be the best in the world. That's what he wanted to be: the best. That's what obsessed him – being the best. What the hell does that mean? It means doing whatever it takes. To anyone. I think he would have done it eventually. He came close a few times.

Maureen: Why Eddie Evans?

Myra: Why not?

Maureen: He weren't a kid.

Myra: Easy as one.

Maureen: What?

Myra: You can't blame me for this one Maureen. Ian picked this one up himself. Hanging around Central station outside the buffet after the bar had shut.

SFX: *Central Station acoustic.*

Myra: He lived in Ardwick.   He'd just come back from Old Trafford. He wasn't waiting for a train.

Maureen: What y' sayin'?

Myra: He were happy enough to come back to our place with Ian.

Maureen: And you.

Myra: Ian told him I was his sister.

Maureen: Ian had met him before.

Myra: So?

Maureen: So that's why he came back with Ian. He just knew him. There's nowt to say he was lookin' for anything.

Myra: I don't know what he was looking for Maureen.

Maureen: Well he wasn't lookin' for a bloody axe in the back of his head.

Myra: Ian said there was something a bit queer about him. That was enough for Ian.

SFX: *Fade acoustic.*

Maureen: My Dave had seen you earlier that night, slinky kinky in your leopard-skin cat-suit.

Myra: It was a dress.

Maureen: Well you'd changed when you came back to our house. Old jumper. Mucky skirt with its ripped hem. You knew then what you were going to do.

Myra: I always wore that for cleaning.

Maureen: Not after that night you didn't. Comin' round after dark. Gettin' us both out of bed just so I could give a message to Mam. Thought it was funny. And you dressed like that, and needing Dave to walk you home. Then you tricked him inside just so he could see you killing Edward Evans.

Myra: Not me. Ian.

Maureen: You were there. The whole time. You watched too.

Myra: Dave joined in.

Maureen: No he didn't.

Myra: He helped clear up.

Maureen: He was terrified. He'd just watched Brady hatchet a man to death and do it so cack-handed that he had to finish him off by twisting an electric flex round his neck.

Ian depicts this in violent action.

Maureen: Then you just cleaned up. As if it were a kids' party.

Ian: Give us a lift, Dave. Eddie's a dead weight.

Ian and Myra find this remark hilarious. Ian exits as if dragging the corpse.

Maureen: And all the while our Gran was upstairs.

Myra: It was her house.

Maureen: She always believed you were innocent.

Myra: It wasn't belief. It was something bigger than that.

Maureen: You ruined so many lives Myra.

Myra: Only because we got caught. And we've got your Dave to thank for that.

Maureen: No, not him. Me. I told him he had to call the police. When he came home he were a wreck. Too scared to do owt. He told me what he'd seen. He wouldn't go out to a 'phone. Not until mornin' when it were light and there were folk knockin' about. When the cops came he couldn't get in the car quick enough. Dave took a knife to protect us and he were that scared they couldn't get it off him. But get this straight Myra, to begin with he were too scared to do owt. He wasn't going to turn you in.

Myra: And you made him?

Maureen: I made him.

Myra: Then you made me.

Maureen: You are getting close Myra, but you're not there yet. (*She collects a camera from the shelves.*)

Myra: What?

Maureen: (SINGS:)

Leave your stepping stones behind, something calls for you

(Don't) Forget the dead you've left, they <u>will</u> follow
you
The vagabond who's rapping at your door
Is standing in the clothes that you once wore
Strike another match, go start anew
And it's all over now, Baby Blue

Maureen takes the infamous mug-shot of Myra as she sings.

Scene Eight: Myra

SFX: Albinoni: *Adagio in G Minor.*

Myra: What's that sound?

Maureen: They'll play it at your funeral.

Myra: When will that be?

Maureen: When you die.

Myra: Have you seen it?

Maureen: Give me chance. I haven't been to my own funeral yet.

Myra: I don't get this haunting business.

Maureen: You'll take to it like a duck to a shiny brook.

Myra: Why have you come, Maureen?

Maureen: Retribution.

Myra: What?

Maureen: Big word. And I didn't learn it in prison.

Myra: This is not you and me, Mo. You've been so nice to me.

Maureen: I am being nice to you.

Myra: It doesn't feel like it.

Maureen: To face what you did is the only chance you have.

Myra: What I didn't do I didn't do.

Maureen: And what you did you did. So why don't you just say it? Say it all.

Myra: There's no more to say.

Maureen: Say it.

Myra: I've said it.

Maureen: Not all of it. Say it.

Myra: I can't say more.

Maureen: Why not?

Myra: Because if I say more they will never let me out of here.

Maureen: Myra, they will never let you out of here.

Myra: Don't.

Maureen: They'll never let you out, Myra. They can't. They will never let you out.

Myra: I don't believe you.

Maureen: I don't believe you.

Myra: For Christ's sake Maureen, can only criminals love me?

Maureen: Ian Brady doesn't love you. He never did.

Myra: He did.

Maureen: He used you. He's still using you, still abusing you.

Myra: Well then he's not the best is he? I'm better

than him, because in spite of all he's done, I loved him. It's easy to love someone lovely, but who can love a monster? Me. Does that make me the best lover in the world? And if so, can anyone love me?

Maureen: You loved a monster, that makes you a monster and if we love you then we become monsters too.

Myra: You love me, Mo, don't you?

SFX: *Fade out the Adagio at the next convenient end of a musical phrase. Meanwhile the actors play out a pause.*

Maureen: I did not laugh for ten years after the night you killed Edward Evans.

Myra: I did not kill him.

Maureen: You swept up bits of his skull. You picked them up with your fingers.

Myra: Try to love me. Love me again. You have loved me.

Maureen: I had no option.

Myra: Neither did I.

Maureen: I divorced Dave and at first I had to refuse to go out with Bill. Why? Because I knew I'd have to tell him I was Myra Hindley's sister.

Myra: Bill's a good man.

Maureen: But even he has been hurt because he dared to love someone who came from the same womb as you.

Myra: And you've got lovely kids. I'm sorry you lost your Dawn, but your Sharon is my ray of sunshine, and she will always be . . . until she's old enough to know who I am.

Maureen: What you are.

Myra: Why 'what'?

Maureen: Because that's what they've made you, Myra. You are not a 'who' any more. You are a 'what'. A thing. An evil thing. If a person can only name one moors murderer, it's you. That's why they'll never let you out.

Myra: Stop saying that.

Maureen: But you know it's true don't you? Nobody wants to be the person who sets Myra Hindley free.

Myra: There are worse than me that have been released. It's just that they are not as well known. I'm reformed, Maureen. Honestly.

Maureen: I don't think so.

Myra: He was a god to me. I had to do what he said.

Maureen: Don't give me that. He may have fooled you into the first one, but you could have gone to the police. You could just have told that copper you were fucking.

Myra: Bog off.

Maureen: It was Pauline, Myra. We both knew her. My Dave had gone out with her. You could have turned Brady in.

Myra: He was my lover.

Maureen: I'm your sister but I turned you in.

Myra: And gave evidence. You wouldn't look at me in court in your nice new coat.

Maureen: And what happened to me? Even my own

family cut me off. You were the fucking murderer and I got cut off. Mum didn't speak to me for five fucking years.

Myra: I was completely under his spell.

Maureen: You bought knives, you bought spades, you bought him his filthy camera, you bought the flaming tape fucking recorder. You listened to it, looked at the photos and got off on them. Then next day you tarted yourself up and went off to work, clocking in as if it was a good morning after a great night out. Meet my sister, short hand typist and child murderer.

Myra: It felt fantastic.

Maureen: He was a psychopath. But you are not. You never were. You are sane. You were always sane.

Myra: Kind of you to say so.

Maureen: No, not kind: true. You are sane, capable, clever. You always were. Clever enough to know not to do it. To stop doing it.

Myra: I was in love!

Maureen: With who?

Myra: With a brilliant psychopath.

Maureen: If you really loved him, you'd have stopped him. You weren't in love with him; you were in love with you.

Myra: Oh fuck off.

Maureen: True, isn't it Myra? "I was in love," you said. "*I* was." "I". That's the important word isn't it? Your love was more important than their lives. Your heartache was more important that their mothers' tears? You never tell the full tale because if you do you will never be free. Your freedom is more important than their little lives.

Myra: It is.

SFX: *Vangelis:* El Greco Movement IX *continue under remaining dialogue:*

Maureen: Well perhaps you'd like to explain that to them.

Myra: What do you mean?

Maureen: You've been talking to me. Talk to them.

Myra: They're here?

Maureen: I didn't say that.

Myra: They can't be here.

Maureen: No. They can't. Because one of them is still missing. Tell us, Myra. Tell us where Keith Bennett is.

Myra: I can't.

Maureen: Won't.

Myra: Ian won't. I can't.

Maureen: Confess to what you – you – actually did. What is there that you haven't told us Myra?

Myra: I've told you all you need to know.

Maureen: We need to know, that you know, what made you what you are.

Myra: The man I loved made me what I am.

Maureen: No, Myra, I think you are wrong.

Myra: If I had not met Ian Brady no one would know my name. And you wouldn't be here.

Maureen: But we are here. Lots of us. Ian Brady didn't change you, Myra.

Myra: Everyone can see that he did.

Maureen: Everyone except me. I knew you before. Nothing about you has changed.

Myra: How can you say that?

Maureen: Because I'm your sister. I knew the child killer when she was a child. You haven't changed at all. And that's your biggest crime. You are clever enough to change. But you won't. Because you are Myra, and Myra won't do anything that Myra doesn't want to do. And Myra doesn't want to undo anything that Myra has done. Because Myra is Myra. Myra is what she is, and whatever she is that's what she will be. And do you know what? Despite everything – prison, hatred, life sentence, abuse, and scorn – I think Myra really loves being Myra.

Myra: Then you don't know me.

Maureen: All of us here know you. And I think we know who made you what you are: you did.

Myra: Listen. I am what I am. But I didn't make me. My mother and father made me; Gorton made me; Ian made me; prison made me; the papers made me; God made me. In his likeness.

Maureen: You made yourself.

Myra: I am not myself.

Maureen: Then who the hell are you?

Myra: A fiction. A tragic heroine. Antigone, Medea, Medusa. The wicked witch. The devil's bitch. I'm the repository of all your deep-rooted, child-scaring psychology. I'm the anti-Christ as created by a million child-molesting journalists. They made me what I am now. I can't un-write myself. I must play out this role for ever. No applause. No final bow. As many encores as you like.

Maureen: Don't look for sympathy Myra, it doesn't suit you.

Myra: Okay. So you've convinced me. I'll live like this 'till I die like this, God help me. But don't tell me it was all me. It can't be all me. There is more to me than your memory of me. Ian made me evil . . .

Maureen: More evil.

Myra: All right, all right – more evil. But it didn't stop there. I've done no more, but you've all made me more evil still. Haven't you? I stopped, but you won't. So who's the best? Who's the best evil person maker: Ian Brady, Myra Hindley or the great British Sun reader? Well, can't you harness your combined superior sanctity and unmake me? Turn me back into someone you can at least share a gutter with?

Maureen: We can't change something that will not change.

Myra: Try me.

Maureen: You will not change. You cannot change. We have not come to make you change.

Myra: Then what the hell do you want to make me do?

Maureen: We want you to admit to being your own creation. To make a full, full confession. To apologise again, and again and again, until there is no apology left in you. To tell all. Tell everything. Every last thing.

Myra: If I do that they will never let me out.

Maureen: They never will let you out. You can't have what you want. For once in your life give other people what we want from you. The details. The whole truth. Tell us please. For them, Myra. For all who knew them. For me.

Myra: I can't.

Maureen: Then we are not going anywhere.

SFX: *Surge soundtrack as Myra stares out as if at the faces of her victims as they return her stare.*

LX: *Slow fade to black*

END

Related events subsequent to the initial performance of this play

Keith's Bennet's mother, Winnie Johnson, died in August 2012 without knowing the location of her son's body, despite a near 50-year campaign to find him and give him a Christian burial. Brady repeatedly refused to say where on Saddleworth Moor he buried Keith.

In 2013 Ian Brady attempted to get himself transferred from a psychiatric hospital to a Scottish prison where he would not be force-fed and could "have control over the manner and timing of his death". His claim to have been on hunger strike for fourteen years was undermined by his barrister, who said he ate toast and soup most days. According to Sefton coroner Christopher Sumner, Brady died of natural causes at 6.02pm on 15th May 2017 aged 79 at Ashworth secure hospital at Maghull, Merseyside. His remains were subsequently secretly cremated and his ashes deposited at sea off Liverpool in the middle of the night.

Discography

Ian Brady marked the murders he committed by giving Myra vinyl records of contemporary hits.

They included:

Theme from The Legion's Last Patrol (composed by Angelo Francesco Lavagnino and performed by Ken Thorne and his Orchestra.)

Twenty-four hours from Tulsa (written by Burt Bacharach and Hal David, sung by Gene Pitney)

It's Over (composed by Roy Orbison and Bill Dees and sung by Roy Orbison)

Girl Don't Come (written by Chris Andrews, sung by Sandie Shaw)

It's All Over Now Baby Blue (written by Bob Dylan sung by Joan Baez)

For her funeral Myra selected:

Adagio in G minor (Albonini)

~

Also available by the same author

The Sherlock Holmes Solution

This is a full-length play for six actors: three females and three males.

This play, which was first performed in 1986 and first published three years later, is an original mystery set in the English county of Lancashire in 1896. The infamous duo of Holmes and Watson are consulted at their Baker Street residence by a factory owner and farmer whose livestock are falling victim to a mysterious fatal illness. On the same day Holmes is visited by a desperate mill worker from the same locality. Her husband was stricken by a strange ailment and now he has disappeared. Holmes realises that the two problems are linked and sets off to solve them. What he finds is the most terrifying threat to himself, and to his reputation, that he has ever had to face.

Peter Hartley provided not only a well-judged plot but a cleverly crafted piece of work that flowed smoothly and sustained the interest.

Lancashire Evening Post, July 1986.

Available from the Amazon kindle store

Will at the Tower

A play and a novel.

You are sixteen, travelling with a companion who is suspected of being a threat to national security, and staying in the houses of religious fundamentalists. Your family and friends have been persecuted and you are uncertain about how brave you can be. Now the authorities are closing in on your latest refuge. The year is 1580, the place is Hoghton Tower, Lancashire, and your name is Will Shakespeare, or Shakspere, or Shakeshaft. It depends on who is asking.

The play is published by *Lazybee Scripts*.

The novel is available from Amazon.

Siren and Saving Grace

Siren is a play for four females and one male. It charts the tale of an American airman based in the UK during the Second World War. The story is told from the perspectives of the two women with whom he corresponded, one in the United States and the other in England. When he fails to return from a mission over Germany, his letters from both women are returned to just one of them. The two meet up twenty years later.

Saving Grace is a play for one performer. Performed on a bare stage with no props, the play recreates the story of Grace Darling (1815 – 1842) who became internationally famous as a consequence of her actions following the wreck of the *Forfarshire* on the Farne Islands in 1838. It also depicts her desperate struggle with the storm of attention she subsequently received during her short life.

This eBook also contains the programme and background material to accompany the 2014 production of Siren, plus *Chaperone* a short fiction to mark the 70th anniversary of the Freckleton Air Disaster.

Available from the Amazon kindle store.

Drama: What it is and How to do it

This book is a no-nonsense guide to creating, rehearsing and staging drama. It focuses on all aspects of acting from your very first encounter with practical drama right through to the final bow at the end of the performance. There is also a major section on how to direct for the stage. It contains chapters on what to expect from drama classes and workshops, and how to devise your own theatre productions. In addition, the book offers some basic definitions of drama and theatre and includes introductions to stage design and producing plays. There is a chapter on professional training and how to approach auditions.

It is an excellent guide for beginners or for more experienced actors who are looking to broaden their range of techniques or progress into directing. It features lots of simple but proven practical tips ranging from how to learn lines to coping with the morning after the closing night.

Available from the Amazon kindle store.

Ice & Lemon

A novel.

Not being able to get his luggage from the plane is the least of Dan's troubles. Heathrow is in a state of chaos. There are lifeless people everywhere but not one bears any sign of trauma or injury. Global communication freezes. London is gridlocked and burning. Mains power fails. Phones fall permanently silent. Life has simply stopped. Only those who were airborne have survived. What has happened? Are his family alive, and can he get to them? And is he as physically unscathed as it seems, or does he carry some hidden legacy of this mysterious, instantaneous catastrophe?

Ice and Lemon chronicles Dan's fraught expedition into a Lancashire blighted by extreme climate and thinly populated by desperate survivors. What he discovers there could have truly cosmic consequences.

Reader reviews:

"An excellent novel. Stunningly assured, gripping from the off."

"Brilliantly told and full of humour and pathos, dealing with grand themes on a localised level."

"The story moves at a tremendous pace with shocks and surprises around every corner and a truly mind blowing conclusion."

Available from the Amazon Kindle Store.

The Atheist's Prayer Book

This is a compendium of short stories in search of the super in the natural.

It is a quest to reveal the spiritual in the secular, the exceptional in the ordinary and the eternal in the momentary. Its blend of orthodox narrative and magical realism cuts into the darkness of misfortune and misadventure to intrigue the thoughtful and enchant the curious.

The prose has been compared to that of Christopher Priest, J.G. Ballard and Alan Garner, and this collection is very much in harmony with the philosophy of the latter, who has suggested that the purpose of stories is in serving *our need to make sense of the natural world and of the hidden forces in ourselves.*

Available from the Amazon Kindle Store.

Christmas Present

Seven seasonal ghost stories.

This Christmas Present is a compendium of seven short ghost stories from northern England. These subtly told tales serve just enough chill to spice up winter evenings by the fireside or lonely commutes during the hours of darkness. Five were first published or broadcast in the 1980s while the opening and closing tales have been crafted especially for this compilation.

Available from the Amazon Kindle Store.

About the author

Pete Hartley is based in northern England where he taught drama for thirty years as well as managing a succession of small fringe production companies specializing in creating new theatre and reworking established classics.

He has written extensively for the stage. Some fifty of his plays have been performed by professionals, amateurs and student companies. Six have won prizes, and one, *Mitigating Circumstances*, was broadcast by BBC Radio.

He has also had short stories published and broadcast and now markets his output under the moniker *uneasybooks*.

24873458R00042

Printed in Poland
by Amazon Fulfillment
Poland Sp. z o.o., Wrocław